TOP HIGH SCHOOL SPORTS

WRESTLING

A Crabtree Branches Book

THOMAS KINGSLEY TROUPE

School-to-Home Support for Caregivers and Teachers

This high-interest book is designed to motivate striving students with engaging topics while building fluency, vocabulary, and an interest in reading. Here are a few questions and activities to help the reader build upon his or her comprehension skills.

Before Reading:

- *What do I think this book is about?*
- *What do I know about this topic?*
- *What do I want to learn about this topic?*
- *Why am I reading this book?*

During Reading:

- *I wonder why...*
- *I'm curious to know...*
- *How is this like something I already know?*
- *What have I learned so far?*

After Reading:

- *What was the author trying to teach me?*
- *What are some details?*
- *How did the photographs and captions help me understand more?*
- *Read the book again and look for the vocabulary words.*
- *What questions do I still have?*

Extension Activities:

- *What was your favorite part of the book? Write a paragraph on it.*
- *Draw a picture of your favorite thing you learned from the book.*

TABLE OF CONTENTS

TAKE IT TO THE MAT!

You struggle to break free from your opponent's hold. Your face is pressed against the mat as time runs out. With a last burst of strength, you break free and pull an amazing reversal. With an arm-bar, you flip your opponent and pin them to the mat. Victory!

Jump into your singlet and strap on your headgear! We're about to learn why wrestling ranks among the… TOP HIGH SCHOOL SPORTS.

FUN FACT

There are three main styles of wrestling: Greco-Roman, freestyle, and folkstyle wrestling, which is the style used in high school wrestling teams.

WRESTLING HISTORY

Wrestling has been part of the world's culture throughout history. Artworks from ancient Babylonia and Egypt show people wrestling, dating back as far as 3000 B.C.E. It was also the most popular sport of the ancient Greeks. Wrestling was included in early Olympic Games and is still part of the Olympics in modern times.

There are many different types of wrestling practiced around the world. The first wrestling tournament was held by the Eastern **Intercollegiate** Wrestling Association in 1905. After that, interest in wrestling grew in colleges and high school.

Cave drawings were discovered showing wrestling moves that are still used today! One of the oldest drawings is over 15,000 years old. It was discovered in a cave in France.

WRESTLING SEASON

For most high schools, the wrestling season starts in late October or early November and continues until February. The number of matches each wrestler will compete in can vary from place to place.

Some places use a point system to determine when the regular season is done for a wrestler. After they reach the point limit, they can only compete in post-season matches.

FUN FACT

The United States wrestling team swept the 1904 Olympics in St. Louis. There were seven freestyle wrestling events and Americans took gold, silver, and bronze in every single event.

HIGH SCHOOL WRESTLING TEAMS

Most high schools have a varsity and a junior varsity wrestling team. Others have even started first-year teams, depending on school size and interest. The varsity team is usually where third- and fourth-year students compete.

Junior varsity is where second-year and sometimes first-year athletes end up. Wrestlers who develop good skills and strength sometimes move up to the varsity level.

Girls high school wrestling teams are becoming more popular in the U.S. and Canada. While other sports were showing decreases, girls wrestling increased by 30 percent in 2018. Nearly half of the states in the U.S. sponsored girls wrestling tournaments in 2019!

BASICS OF THE SPORT

Wrestling can be a difficult sport to understand at first. A high school wrestling match consists of three two-minute periods. The goal is to score as many points as possible during the periods.

If a wrestler manages to pin their opponent at any time before the end of the third period, it's an automatic win!

FUN FACT

Some National Football League (NFL) Hall of Fame athletes were once high school wrestlers. Baltimore Ravens linebacker Ray Lewis was a two-time high school state champion in Florida. Los Angeles/Oakland Raiders offensive guard Steve Wisniewski was a state champion in California.

WEIGHT CLASSES

Though wrestling is a team sport in high school, the wrestler on the mat is on his or her own. The way that they determine how to match up wrestlers with another opponent is by weight.

WRESTLING WEIGHT CLASSES (IN POUNDS)

BOYS	GIRLS
106	101
113	106
120	111
126	116
132	121
138	126
145	131
152	137
160	143
170	150
182	160
195	170
220	189
285	235

No wrestler is expected to **grapple** on the mat with someone who weighs more than they do and vice versa. To compete at the different weight classes, wrestlers eat right and exercise to make sure they can make weight.

In the U.S., high school wrestling weight classes went through a significant change in 2012. The National Federal High School Association (NFHS) adjusted the classes after looking at data from 200,000 wrestlers from across the country. The goal was to help ensure that around seven percent of all wrestlers are represented in each weight class.

WRESTLING POSITIONS

Wrestling positions work differently than positions in other sports. In wrestling, the position is where the wrestler is in relation to their opponent.

Top Position (Referee Position) — In this position, the wrestler is above an opponent and in control.

Neutral Position — This is the starting position where the wrestler stands face to face with an opponent. It is hardest to score points from this position, but neither wrestler is at an advantage or disadvantage.

Bottom Position (Referee Position) — In this position, the wrestler is on their hands and knees, with the opponent wrapped above them.

BOTTOM POSITION

If the wrestlers end up out of the ring, the referee will reset them in the middle. They will be positioned as they were when they left the ring.

THE BASIC MOVES

There are many of techniques available to use during a wrestling match. Below are some of the most common ones.

arm bar — wrapping an arm around an opponent's elbow and using the **leverage** to flip them over

cross-face — a hold where the wrestler's arm is pressed to their opponent's face

grapple — grasping an opponent with hands to control and execute wrestling **maneuvers**

half (or full) nelson — a hold where the wrestler's arm locks the opponent's head into position through the armpit and a hand is placed at the back of their head

reversal — moving from the bottom position into the controlling top position

takedown — taking an opponent down to the mat from the neutral position

ARM BAR

CROSS-FACE

GRAPPLE

NELSON

TAKEDOWN

Though it may not look like it, wrestling isn't just a free-for-all. There are a number of illegal moves that can disqualify or even ban wrestlers from ever competing again. It's illegal to pinch or poke an opponent with fingers, toes, or nails. That also means no "fish-hooking" the opponent's mouth or nose. Eye-gouges are a quick way to end a wrestling career. Keep it clean!

EQUIPMENT AND UNIFORMS

High school wrestling is a contact sport, which can lead to injuries. To protect their ears, wrestlers wear headgear, secured with a chin strap. Mouth-guards protect their teeth.

The uniform is either the traditional one-piece singlet, or a **compression** tank top and shorts. Wrestlers also wear wrestling shoes that look like high-tops to help them maneuver on the mat.

FUN FACT

Red and green anklets are usually worn around a wrestler's ankle. These are used to designate who is who when a referee signals points that are scored during a match.

PRACTICE AND TRAINING

Most high school wrestling practices are held after school, but many wrestlers train all year. Many do heavy weight training in the off-season to build muscle. During wrestling season, they do training to keep their muscles strong and prevent being sore during practices.

During practice, wrestlers work on skills, including grappling, slams, and holds. **Stamina** in wrestling is extremely important. Most coaches push their team to run and build up their endurance, or ability to last a long time.

WRESTLING JARGON

Like most sports, wrestling uses its own language of terms and phrases that might confuse athletes new to the sport! Here are some to get you started:

Backdoor — to slip between an opponent's legs when in the bottom position

Bridge — lifting the back up to avoid being pinned to the mat

Gassed — running out of energy during a match

Made weight — when a wrestler weighs in for a match and is approved to wrestle in that weight class

Over/under — lock up where a wrestler has one arm wrapped over and the other arm under the opponent's arm

Whizzer — a clinch hold used to control an opponent where the wrestler puts an arm over the opponent's arm and **encircles** the opponent's arm or upper body

BACKDOOR

GASSED

BRIDGE

STATE TOURNAMENTS

High school wrestling teams face off against nearby schools to determine who the best is. Teams that perform well during the season can participate in state championships and tournaments.

FUN FACT

The first United States wrestling tournament was held in New York City in 1888.

As with most sports, wrestling teams are divided into classes determined by the number of students the high school has. The classes ensure that big schools compete with big schools and don't have an unfair advantage over small schools.

CONCLUSION

Wrestling is one of the most difficult and demanding sports high-schoolers can compete in. It takes hard work, quick thinking, and endurance to rule the mat. Fans never see the same wrestling match twice!

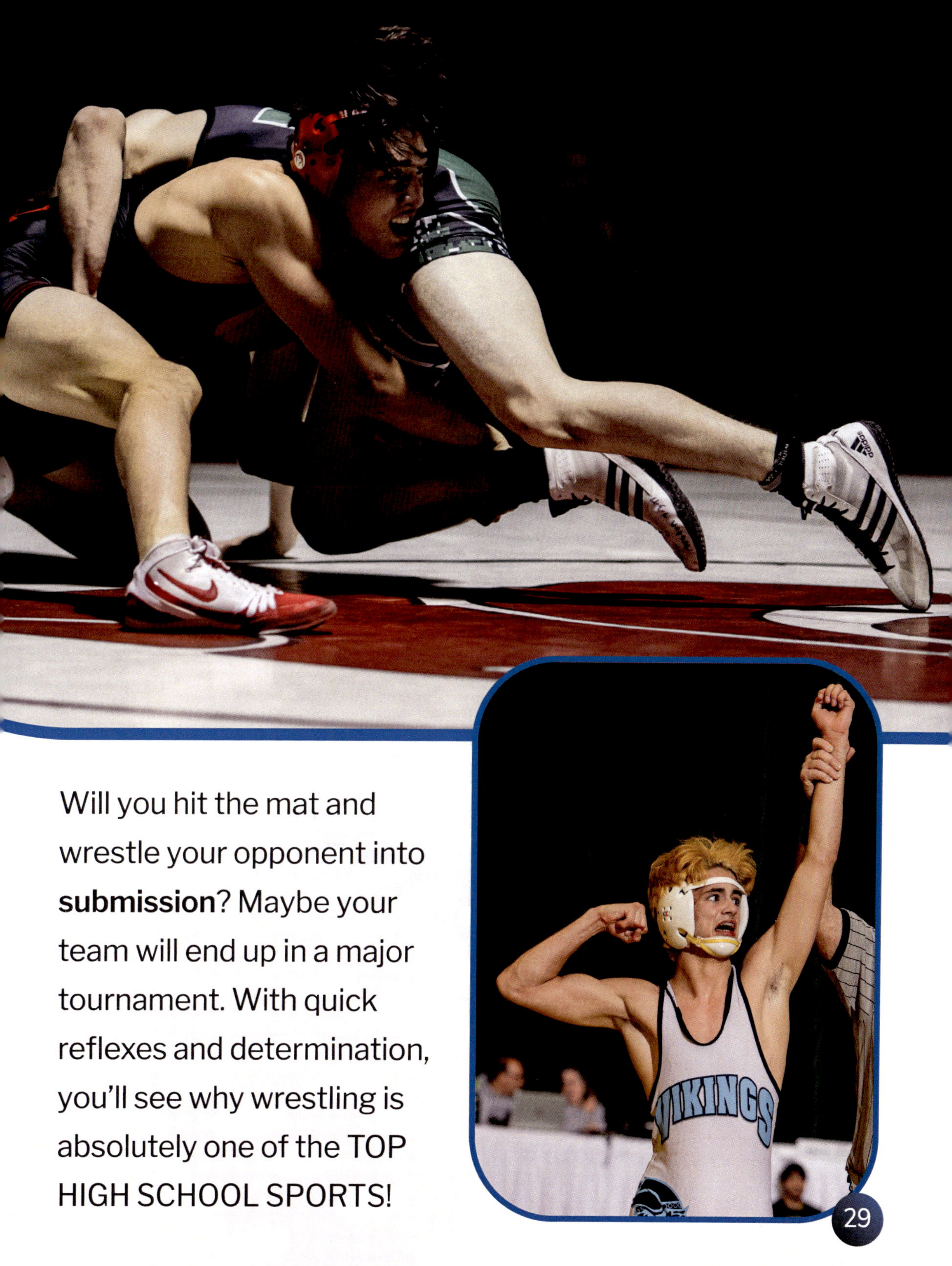

Will you hit the mat and wrestle your opponent into **submission**? Maybe your team will end up in a major tournament. With quick reflexes and determination, you'll see why wrestling is absolutely one of the TOP HIGH SCHOOL SPORTS!

GLOSSARY

compression (KUHM-press-uhn): the act of pressing or squeezing something

disqualify (diss-KWOL-uh-FYE): ban from competing for violating a rule

encircles (en-SUR-kuhlz): forms a circle around or surrounds

grapple (GRAP-uhl): a close fight or struggle without weapons

intercollegiate (in-tur-kol-EE-juht): existing between colleges or universities

leverage (LEV-ur-ij): use of force to move an object

maneuvers (muhn-OO-verz): a series of moves that require skill

sponsored (SPON-surd): to provide funding or money to an organization

stamina (STAM-i-nuh): ability to keep using physical or mental effort

submission (suhb-MISH-uhn): accepting defeat or surrendering to an opponent

INDEX

WEBSITES TO VISIT

https://kids.kiddle.co/Wrestling

https://www.softschools.com/facts/sports/wrestling_facts/796/

https://kids.britannica.com/kids/article/wrestling/353938

ABOUT THE AUTHOR

Thomas Kingsley Troupe

Thomas Kingsley Troupe is the author of a big ol' pile of books for kids. He's written about everything from ghosts to Bigfoot to third grade werewolves. He even wrote a book about dirt. When he's not writing or reading, he gets plenty of exercise and remembers sacking quarterbacks while on his high school football team. Thomas lives in Woodbury, Minnesota with his two sons.

Crabtree Publishing

crabtreebooks.com 800-387-7650

Hardcover	978-1-0396-4604-9
Paperback	978-1-0396-4731-2
Ebook (pdf)	978-1-0396-5208-8
Epub	978-1-0396-5415-0
Read-along	978-1-0396-5622-2
Audio book	978-1-0396-5904-9

Printed in the U.S.A./072025/CP20250722

Library and Archives Canada Cataloguing in Publication
Available at the Library and Archives Canada

Library of Congress Cataloging-in-Publication Data
Available at the Library of Congress

Published in Canada
Crabtree Publishing
616 Welland Avenue
St. Catharines, Ontario
L2M 5V6

Published in the United States
Crabtree Publishing
347 Fifth Avenue
Suite 1402-145
New York, NY 10016

Written by: Thomas Kingsley Troupe
Designed by: Jennifer Dydyk
Edited by: Kelli Hicks
Proofreader: Ellen Rodger

Photographs: Following images from Shutterstock.com: Cover background pattern (and pattern throughout book © HNK, wrestling gear in background on cover and title page © Praneat, cover photos of wrestlers © JoeSAPhotos. Page 8 © baranq, Page 11 bottom photo © JoeSAPhotos, Page 12 bottom photo and Page 13 © Ahturner, Page 14 wrestler in background© Skeronov, wrestler in foreground © Everyonephoto Studio, Page 20 and 23 © Ahturner, Page 22 © Ben Gingell. Following image from istock by Getty Images: Page 6 © Zzvet. Following images from Dreamstime.com: Pages 4, 5, 9 © Michael Turner, Page 10 © Vitalij Sova, Page 11 top photo © Jon Osumi, Page 12 top photo © Ericfehrenbacher, Page 15 © Vitalij Sova, Page 17 and 19 all images © Michael Turner except cross-face image © Jon Osumi, Page 21 top photo © Michael Turner, bottom photo © Jon Osumi, Page 25 top photo © Michael Turner, bottom two photos © Susan Leggett, Page 26 Jon Osumi, Page 27 top photo © Susan Leggett, bottom photo © Michael Turner, Page 28 and Page 29 all photos © Michael Turner. Page 7 bottom public domain photo from Wikimedia, top photo courtesy of the Library of Congress.